My Work for Me

Written by Deborah Plona Cerbus
& Cheryl Feichtenbiner Rice
Adapted by Dona Rice
Illustrated by Sue Fullam

All my five senses
help me know
About the world
 in which I grow.

I use my eyes
　　so I can see
The sky, the clouds,
　　a bird, a bee.

With both my ears
I clearly hear
All kinds of sounds,
both far and near.

Day in, day out,
I use my nose.
Do I smell pickles
or a rose?

My hungry tongue
tastes what I eat.
Does food taste sour?
Salty? Sweet?

I like my fingers
   very much.
I need them for
   my sense of touch.

I do so many things,
    you see,
Because my senses
    work for me.

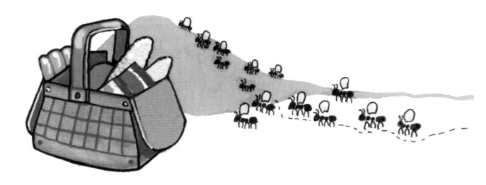

All my five senses help me know
About the world in which I grow.